THE TRUE STORY OF SANTA CLAUS

Written and illustrated by

Paul Prokop

Pauline
BOOKS & MEDIA

Library of Congress Cataloging-in-Publication Data

Prokop, Paul.
The true story of Santa Claus / written and illustrated by Paul Prokop.
p. cm.
Summary: A child learns that Santa Claus is really Saint Nicholas, a bishop who lived long ago and taught people about Jesus. Includes information about the evolution of the gift-giving Santa Claus.
ISBN 0-8198-7406-X (pbk.)
1. Nicholas, Saint, Bp. of Myra—Juvenile literature. [1. Nicholas, Saint, Bp. of Myra. 2. Saints. 3. Santa Claus. 4. Christmas. 5. Holidays. 6. Jesus Christ. 7. Christian life.] I. Title.
BR1720.N46 P76 2000
242'.335—dc21

00-008967

Printed and published in the U.S.A. by Pauline Books & Media, 50 Saint Pauls Avenue, Boston, MA 02130-3491.

www. pauline.org

Pauline Books & Media is the publishing house of the Daughters of St. Paul, an international congregation of women religious serving the Church with the communications media.

3 4 5 6 7 07 06 05 04 03 02

For
Mary, Peter, Hannah,
and Daniel Nicholas

It was the night before Christmas, and Nicholas was in bed. He wasn't too sure what sugarplums were, but there weren't any dancing in *his* head, because he was awake.

For several years now, Santa Claus had been able to sneak into Nicholas's house on Christmas Eve. Santa always brought wonderful treats and presents. But he always came while Nicholas was sleeping and left before Nicholas woke up. *This year,* Nicholas decided, *I'm going to see Santa Claus with my very own eyes!*

So...he waited until he was pretty sure his mom and dad were asleep. Then he crept very quietly out of his bedroom and down the stairs to the living room.

Now, Nicholas was a little afraid of the dark. So he was glad that his parents always kept the tree lit on Christmas Eve...for Santa Claus. His tiger was glad too!

Nicholas climbed onto the couch next to the decorated tree. He crawled under the cozy Christmas quilt his grandma had made. He sniffed the sweet pine smell of the Christmas tree. The lights on the tree cast magical patterns on the walls of the room. Nicholas felt warm and comforted in their glow.

Nicholas tried to keep his mind busy so that he could stay awake.... But just as he heard the mantle clock chime many times (maybe it was twelve), Nicholas drifted off to sleep.

He dreamed of a crisp winter night. The moon shone brightly upon a forest of pine trees and frost-covered mountains. Snowflakes drifted down like tiny white feathers from heaven. Nicholas heard a faraway sound like the jingling of sleigh bells. He saw something flying over the mountains in the distant night sky.

The sound of the jingling bells came closer and closer. Suddenly it was so close and so real that it woke him up!

Nicholas blinked. He rubbed his eyes. It seemed unbelievable, but sitting beside him on the couch was Santa Claus himself! He was wearing his warm red coat and hat, and munching on the cookies Nicholas's mom had left him. Dangling from the tip of his hat was a tiny golden bell. It jingled happily whenever he moved.

"Merry Christmas, sleepy head!" Santa chuckled.

Nicholas was really surprised. He was so surprised, in fact, that he could hardly answer. "M-M-Merry Christmas," he finally stuttered.

"It's well past your bedtime, Nicholas," Santa observed. (How he knew this, he didn't say.) "But since you're still awake, maybe you can help me unload my sack."

Nicholas slid off the couch and reached into the big bag. He pulled out a beautifully wrapped gift for his mom. The next one was for his dad. Then came several brightly colored packages marked: *For Nicholas from Santa.*

Nicholas and Santa Claus carefully placed all the presents under the Christmas tree. Then Nicholas helped Santa finish off his mom's homemade cookies.

When the cookies were all gone, Santa said, "It's time you got to bed, young man. It's getting very late."

"Oh, no!" Nicholas almost shouted. "Now I'm too excited to go to sleep!"

Santa thought for a moment. "Do you think a bedtime story might do the trick?"

"Yes!" Nicholas exclaimed. "Please tell me a story about *you*!"

"Very well," said Santa. "I'll tell you the *true* story of Santa Claus."

Grinning from ear to ear, Nicholas eagerly climbed into Santa Claus's lap. Then Santa began: "Once upon a time, there was *another* little boy named Nicholas..."

"Like me?" asked Nicholas. "Was he a friend of yours?"

"You could say that," replied Santa as he stroked his beard. "But Nicholas's *best* friend was Jesus, the Son of God. Nicholas's parents taught him all about Jesus. They told Nicholas that God sent His Son into the world as a little baby on the very first Christmas. They told him that Jesus was born in a stable under the light of a star in Bethlehem."

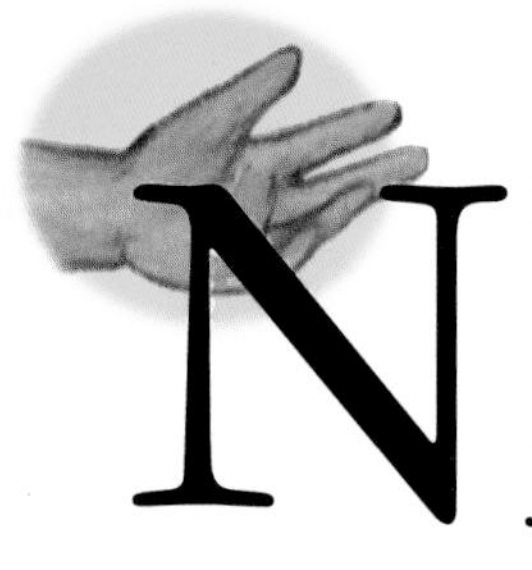

Nicholas prayed every night to Jesus. He asked Jesus to help him to always do what was right. Nicholas promised Jesus that he would spend his life doing God's work.

"Nicholas never forgot his promise as he grew up and became a man. He was always helping others and teaching them about God our Father and His Son, Jesus.

"He told everyone that God so loved the world that He sent us His only Son as a little baby on that first Christmas day. He taught people that when Jesus grew up, He showed His great love for us by dying on the cross to save us from our sins. Then Jesus rose from the dead so that we might live forever with Him in heaven.

"Nicholas paid special attention to the children. He played games with them in the streets of the town. He told them stories about Jesus. And he told them all about God's wonderful love and care for each one of them.

"The children knew that Nicholas was their friend. They trusted him. And they felt the love of Jesus coming to them through him."

The people of the town saw how much Nicholas loved God. After a while, they chose him to lead them as their bishop.

"As bishop, Nicholas made sure that everyone knew the truth about God. He also used his own money to help the poor people of the town.

"When Nicholas heard about a very poor family, he would secretly go to their home in the middle of the night. Then he would toss a bag of gold coins in through an open window or down the chimney."

Sometimes, Nicholas would walk through the streets of the town bringing small gifts in Jesus' name to the poorest children. He wanted the children to have hope and to know that God really loved each of them.

"Nicholas spent his whole life serving God and his people. God made it possible for Nicholas to cure sick children, and to work many other miracles as signs of God's love.

"Through Nicholas, God helped many people to believe in His Son Jesus."

Then, one cold winter night, when Nicholas had grown very old, he said his prayers and got ready to go to bed. Just as he was about to fall asleep, the Child Jesus miraculously appeared to him. Nicholas was so surprised he couldn't even speak.

"Jesus smiled and said, 'You have made me very happy, Nicholas. You have brought God's love to the people of your town. Many people have come to know and love me because of you. You have taught everyone to be as loving and trusting as little children, just as my Father wants them to be. You are my good and faithful servant. But now your work here is finished. It is time for you to come with me and live forever in my Father's house.'

"'But Lord, there is so much yet to be done,' Nicholas replied. 'Who will teach the children? Who will look after them?'

"'*You* will,' said Jesus. 'Now you will look after the children of the whole world until the end of time.'"

And then, on that cold winter night, the Child Jesus took Nicholas by the hand and led him home to His heavenly kingdom.

"From that time on, Nicholas has done what Jesus asked. He joyfully looks after the children of the whole world. He watches over them from heaven. And on one special night every year, Nicholas brings the love of the Child Jesus to all those who celebrate His birth on that first Christmas day.

"The children of the world now call Nicholas by many names. But the name he is most proud of is that of *Saint*...or as it is said in some places, *Santa.*"

"He's *you!*" cried the little boy in Santa's lap. "Nicholas is *you!*"

"That's right," nodded Santa with a big smile. "And now that you know the *real* reason I visit on Christmas Eve, I want you to do something for me. Always remember that Jesus, who came to earth on that very first Christmas, is God's most special gift of love to us. And God wants you to pass on that love to everyone you meet.... Most of all, treasure Jesus who lives in your heart. Remember that He promises to be with you always, even until the end of time."

Nicholas promised to do just that. And before Santa could say another word, Nicholas threw his arms around the jolly saint's neck, and gave him a big tiger hug. (That's like a bear hug, only TIGHTER.)

Then Nicholas quietly tiptoed back upstairs to his soft, warm bed. And *Saint* Nicholas left to continue his long winter night of travels.

And so, on a Christmas Eve not so very long ago, a little boy named Nicholas finally went to sleep. Visions of Baby Jesus and the warm glow of God's love were dancing in his head…

And what's this?… Those must be sugarplums!

More about Saint Nicholas

Saint Nicholas lived in the fourth century A.D., and was the bishop of Myra in Asia Minor. He was well known for his holiness and his generosity to the poor, and also for being a fierce defender of the true Christian faith. He had a great reputation for working miracles in the name of Jesus Christ. Some stories even say that he brought children back to life.

Saint Nicholas was imprisoned for preaching Christianity during the persecution carried out by the Roman emperor Diocletian, but was released when Constantine made Christianity legal in the Roman Empire. He was present at the Council of Nicaea in 325 A.D., at which he strongly denounced the Arian heresy.

The name of Saint Nicholas has been invoked by many of the faithful for centuries, and he is the patron saint of children. Saint Nicholas was famous for giving gifts, especially to the poor and to those in trouble. It is this reputation that is the source of his association with gift giving at Christmas. Saint Nicholas's name was transformed by the Dutch to *Sinter Klaas,* and finally to *Santa Claus.* His feast day is celebrated on December 6.

It is difficult to separate fact from legend regarding the life of Saint Nicholas. But we can be sure of one thing: Saint Nicholas is alive and well and living in the glorious company of the Risen Christ, where he enjoys the promise of the resurrection that awaits all those who love the Lord.

MERRY CHRISTMAS!